Looking Good

MANNERS

by Judy Klare

Rourke Publications, Inc.
Vero Beach, FL 32964

Julia Klare was born in Colony, Kansas. Mrs. Klare took her B.A. in Elementary Education in Kansas City and her M.A. in Counseling Psychology at the University of Minnesota. She is a teacher and a licensed psychologist.

Library of Congress Cataloging-in-Publication Data

Klare, Judith, 1922-
   Manners / by Judy Klare.
      p.   cm. — (Looking good)
   Includes bibliographical references.
   Summary: Discusses the importance of good manners
and provides suggestions for appropriate behavior in various
situations.
   1. Etiquette for children and teenagers. [1. Etiquette.]
I. Title. II. Series: Looking good (Vero Beach, Fla.)
BJ1857.C5K57   1990   90-31638
395′.122—dc 20   CIP
ISBN 0-86625-419-6   AC

CONTENTS

WHAT IS ETIQUETTE?

Have you ever been in a situation where you knew something was expected of you, but you had no idea what it was? There you were, the center of attention, and you were at a loss for just the right word or gesture. Yet, what you say and do in social situations reveals a lot about the person you are and the person you wish to be.

For generations, parents have said, "Mind your manners." You may have wondered what they meant by this often repeated warning. The rules of behavior your parents live by may seem meaningless, cumbersome, or just plain confusing. Why bother with all this, anyway? What is etiquette?

Etiquette, for most of us, is difficult to define. A French word, it means "conduct required by good breeding or prescribed by those in authority." This definition raises two questions. What is "good breeding?" and who are "those in authority?" Answers to these questions could be debated. Most people agree, however, that the most important rule of etiquette is to **treat others as you want to be treated**. That idea is the basis for all the rules in all the etiquette books ever written.

Think about it. Don't you want others to treat you the way they themselves want to be treated? If friends, teachers, brothers, sisters, parents, and store clerks treated you with this principle in mind, wouldn't life be a lot easier and more pleasant? And wouldn't life be a lot more pleasant for them if you lived according to this idea, too?

Knowing the rules of etiquette can sometimes help things go more smoothly, but rules by themselves are empty. Rules cover specific occasions; they may even change from time to time. Knowing the *reasons* for good manners (like understanding the basics of arithmetic) makes it easier to use them on a daily basis.

With children and teens, "be seen and not heard" used to be the rule, but customs have changed and ideas about what is or is not acceptable have become more flexible. This does not mean that manners are no longer important. In fact, they are more important than ever because more privilege means more responsibility. **Using good manners shows that you have the maturity to realize that other people have rights and needs that must be respected**. In return, expressing this basic principle can give *you* confidence in all kinds of situations. It will help overcome shyness as well. You will not have to shrink into the woodwork because *you* don't know what to do or say. Good manners are for *everyday* and *all* occasions.

6

Why Be Polite, Anyway?

What is the payoff to **you** in learning to be polite? Being familiar with agreed-upon rules of etiquette can:

> boost your self-esteem (how you like yourself).
>
> help you meet your own needs, without putting others down.
>
> make a good impression on the people in your life, such as family, girlfriends, teachers, boyfriends, (and later) employers.

At first glance, a connection between your manners and your self-esteem may seem remote. When you practice good manners at every opportunity, however, your reputation as a thoughtful, considerate person begins to grow. Usually you can expect to receive mannerly treatment in return. How people treat you **does** affect your self-esteem. Being treated well improves your feelings about yourself. It almost goes without saying that self-esteem can suffer otherwise. All this doesn't happen overnight, but it **does happen**.

Practicing good manners means that good manners will begin to come naturally. You will not even have to think about them. You will just **know** how to behave. This eventually will carry over even into more difficult social situations than the ones already discussed.

We live in a complex world; therefore, everyone may not agree on the best way to behave on every occasion. For this reason, all of us need to learn and practice those rules of etiquette that most people do agree on. It is also a good idea to re-think the purposes behind these rules.

Common Sense Guidelines

Wait your turn to speak rather than interrupt when another person is speaking.

Use the word "please" when asking for someone's help, and respond with "thank you" when the help is given. Say, "No, thank you" when refusing an offer of help or food from someone.

Be as polite at home as you are when you are a guest in someone else's house. Your family deserves your best manners.

Be aware of the privacy needs of others. Knock before entering a room, and avoid listening in on private conversations.

Show respect for older persons.

In general, answer rudeness with politeness. Practice this rule in school, in your family, with clerks, on the phone, anywhere. It can result in better feelings all around; you may also get better service. Remember that the rudeness may not be directed at you. It may arise from something going on in the other person's head.

When you share space with others — in a family, dorm, summer camp, anywhere — do your part to take care of the things you use. Clean the tub after bathing. Tidy the kitchen after snacks. Store your own things.

Make family dinners pleasant, relaxing occasions. Don't fight with brothers and sisters. Keep the conversation upbeat and interesting.

Avoid holding a conversation with one person if it appears that a third person will then be left out.

Offer to help your parents with chores. Happy parents are a lot easier to live with than tired, stressed-out ones.

Even though there may be agreement on this list, it does not begin to cover ALL the daily occasions that call for good manners. So, what is the answer? How can you be expected to develop social skills if clear rules don't exist for all occasions?

Here's one, surefire rule for all occasions: No matter how other things may change, treating others as you wish to be treated is the most basic and important rule of etiquette. This one rule never changes, and it makes most situations easier.

How would you deal with the episodes below?

A long time ago, you accepted an invitation to go to a play. Recently you were invited to a party that will take place on the same night and at the same time.

a. Keeping others' feelings in mind, I must go to the play; I can explain to the party-giver that I accepted the other invitation first.

b. I think it would be best not to go to either function.

c. I'd rather go to the party; I'll make up some excuse to get out of going to the play. My date for the play doesn't know about the party so he won't know I'm lying.

The first solution is the best one. The second is a cop-out. The third is likely to get you into trouble sooner or later.

You have a seat on a crowded bus. An elderly man boards the bus.

a. Since I am a girl, I don't need to give up my seat.

b. Girl or boy doesn't matter; I will offer him my seat.

Leave gender out of this. Young people of either sex offer their seats to an elderly person.

It is a very warm day in April. You are wearing white sandals. Your aunt tells you that, in her day, no one wore white shoes until June 1st. How do you reply?

a. "What a quaint idea!"

b. "With the weather this warm, it just seems appropriate."

c. "And in your day, everyone also wore corsets and bloomers . . . Ugh!"

10

The second response is neutral. The first and third ridicule your aunt's ideas. Even if her comments to you implied criticism, answering with ridicule will not help to change her into a smiling, uncritical auntie.

The Christmas sweater you received from your grandmother is not your size or style. How do you thank her?

a. Enthusiastically, but don't go overboard.

b. To spare her feelings later, you explain you would like to exchange it for one you liked from the same store.

c. When she asks if you like it, stall.

This is a toughie, but you can never go wrong on the first response. What you say next, if anything, depends on your relationship with your grandmother, whether or not she lives nearby, if she has included a sales slip for exchange, etc. A gift should always be received with enthusiasm. After all, it is a gift.

You are at a friend's for supper. The family is used to saying a prayer before meals. Your family does not have this custom.

a. You explain that your family doesn't do this.

b. You show respect by bowing your head along with the others.

It isn't necessary to explain your family's behavior. Do as you would do when attending a church service of another faith. Out of respect, you would most likely follow the lead of others who are participating.

In the above examples, the payoff to you may not happen right away. You will, however, come across as a person who respects others' needs, but who also is confident and proud of herself.

COMMUNICATING YOUR IDEAS

All your life, you'll be dealing with people. Knowing how to handle social situations will help you feel comfortable and poised in every situation.

The Telephone

Telephones are a fact of life in the twentieth century. They are both a curse and a blessing. Here are some ideas for handling the more stressful phone dilemmas.

Wrong number. No question about it, wrong numbers are irritating — to both parties. If you are the caller, it helps to say you are sorry. If you receive the call, it does not help to give an angry response, even if you feel angry.

No answer. Let the phone ring at least seven or eight times (up to ten). The person you are calling may not be able to answer sooner, so give him or her a chance to get to the phone.

Late-night call. A call at such a time may be necessary. The caller may have important news that cannot wait. If you receive such a call, you may have to take down certain information. Try to be courteous and helpful, even if you are upset. You may have to wake other family members. Try to do this calmly. If the news is bad, your self-control and understanding can help. If the news is good, self-control is also likely to be helpful.

Inconvenient call. Ask if you have called at a busy time. It could be mealtime; the doorbell might just have rung; or others may be waiting to use the phone. Be sure to call back if you are asked to. If someone calls when *you* cannot talk, say so up front, and offer to call back at a more convenient time.

Answering machine. Make your message brief. Include only needed details. Give the date, time of day, or both, if appropriate. If you dislike talking to a machine, try to imagine the person you are calling as you speak. Do not give up after the beep!

A child answers. Depending on the child's age, you may need to persuade him or her to get an adult to take a message. Be patient. Young children may need to practice in order to be trusted on the phone later on. If you are a friend or relative, you may enjoy helping. At any rate, an adult may be close by to help the child take your message.

> **TIP**: If you are the one in charge, do not let very young children answer the phone without someone responsible being nearby. You run the risk of a message not being relayed. A playful child may also be irritating to a caller in a hurry.

Obscene call. In the case of an obscene call, hang up quickly. Do not reply. If the caller is threatening or there are many such calls, notify the police. You can also ask the phone company for advice. (Look in the front section of your telephone directory for the number.) Remember, you are protected from nuisance calls under state and federal laws.

An important phone call comes for a family member who is out.

Answering the phone for someone who is not there is a common problem requiring good manners. Suppose you're home alone. The phone rings and you answer, but it's not a familiar voice. The caller sounds hurried and also disappointed that the person he wanted cannot be reached. How do you respond to this kind of call?

Offer to take the message. Sound helpful and interested. No paper or pencil by the phone? Politely ask the caller to wait until you get some. Take the caller's name and number. Read them back if you're not sure. You might also include the time of the call. Even if you have business of your own to take care of, stay on the line until you have all the information you need. **No matter how — or how often — he or she asks, never tell a stranger that you are home alone.**

14

Letter Writing

The art of letter writing has gone into decline in recent years. But don't bury the corpse yet! The gracious letter, like all the mannerly arts, is staging a rebirth. Of course, you know that you should send out your "thank-yous" promptly, but what happens if you just plain forget?

Your reply is late. If you've procrastinated, the best way out is to make a brief apology, and then go on with your letter. If you spend too long on your apology, you won't have any space left for news!

Writing to a boyfriend. Be sincere, but avoid being too gushy. If you miss him, say so, but do not try to make him feel guilty for not being with you. Avoid trying to make him feel jealous by mentioning your busy social schedule. Think of several interesting or amusing things to say.

A "thank-you" to someone you don't know. Mention that you have never met, if that's the case. If she or he does not know your town or area, a brief item or two about your town can be included. The purpose is the thank-you, so don't feel you have to write a novelette!

> **TIP**: The easiest way to write most letters is to imagine that you are talking with the person. Say what you might say if you were face-to-face.

Using "Ms." correctly. Whether a woman is married, single, or divorced, "Ms." is appropriate when used in the address on a letter. However, when you think a particular woman might feel more comfortable with the old forms ("Mrs." or "Miss"), use them. Don't use "Mrs." unless you are sure the woman is married and prefers to be called "Mrs."

Introductions

Here are some points to remember when introducing one person to another.

A friend to an older person. You say, "Mrs. Carter, this is my friend, Betty Jo Newcomb." Then say, "Betty Jo, I'd like you meet Mrs. Carter." (You say the older person's name first because you are presenting the YOUNGER person TO the OLDER person.)

A stranger to a relative; a man to a woman. Say, "Aunt Jane, I want you to meet Mr. Wrigley, my science teacher." Then say, "Mr. Wrigley, this is Mrs. Roosevelt, my aunt." (You say your relative's name first because you are presenting a STRANGER TO a RELATIVE, and a MAN TO a WOMAN.)

A stepparent. A stepfather or stepmother ordinarily will not be insulted if you call them just that: "my stepfather," "my stepmother." Most other titles (for example, "my father's wife" or "my mother's husband") can be unnecessarily awkward. Use your best judgment.

When you can't remember a name. When introducing a person whom you have met only recently, you might say, "Please tell me your name again." When introducing a friend or an acquaintance whose name you cannot recall at that moment, apologize briefly, ask for the name, and go on with the introduction.

Introducing yourself. Say, "I am . . . (first and last name)," then offer your hand and shake the hand offered you.

TIP: A handshake is important to an introduction. Shake hands with friendly vigor
but, at the same time, don't overdo it.
If your handshake is firm, you come
across as confident, likable, friendly.
A "wet-fish" handshake doesn't make
a strong impression.

Staying Over

A pleasant, considerate guest is asked back again. Acting bossy, antisocial, or sloppy is a sure way to get dropped from the guest list.

When you are late. If you are late, an apology is in order. Otherwise, your friend's parents may worry needlessly. If possible, call when you see you are running late. Leave a message, if necessary. Even if you think your call may wake someone, it is probably wise to call anyway. You must decide this one.

Fancy towels. Go ahead and use a fancy towel unless you have been told to use other towels. If you do use a fancy towel, hang it back in a way that shows it has been used. Otherwise, the hostess won't know you've used it.

Asked to watch a show. In someone else's home, you should watch the program suggested, even if you are not particularly interested. If you do have strong feelings against the program, it is all right to ask to be excused, but do this without putting down others' opinions. You will have to judge the situation yourself. Your response depends on how well you know your host family's attitudes, or they yours.

TIP: Above all, do not interrupt while a person is obviously watching TV. This is not an appropriate time or way to express your opinion of the program.

You're short on cash. Be frank if you are caught short. The money you brought may not cover an unexpected lunch and a swim or an extra movie. In any case, try to discuss your finances in advance.

Unsure of house rules. Ask if you have any questions about rules. It is perfectly all right to inquire about what is expected of you.

Clean up your messes. Nobody wants to be your personal maid! A welcome guest leaves no messes.

Be polite. Treat everyone in the family — including little brothers and sisters — in a mannerly way.

Dining Out

Dining out deserves a whole etiquette book in itself. Remember what we said about consideration for others? It applies to dining out, too. Here are some special hints.

Menu hard to understand. Many menus contain French, Italian, or Spanish words. It is all right to ask your waiter or waitress for help. To prepare yourself, the guide to menus on page 20 will help you pronounce some foreign menu words, and will tell you what they mean. Most English dictionaries also include lists of foreign phrases.

To split a dessert. If you'd like to split a dessert, ask. Waiters are used to this request.

You are dissatisfied. Tell the person who is serving you about it quietly. She/he can handle it.

A Guide to Menus and Other Restaurant Lore

à la carte (ah lah CART) — you pay one price for the main dish and extra for *any other* items

à la mode (ah lah MODE) — topped with ice cream

bouillon (BOO yawn) — a clear beef-tasting soup; is also made of chicken; usually served hot

consomme (CON so MAY) — a clear, well-seasoned soup; is sometimes jellied and served cold

crepe (KREPP) — a very thin pancake wrapped around meat, fish or cheese; when wrapped around fruits, served as a dessert

fettucini (FEH too CHEE nee) — narrow ribboned pasta

entrée (ON tray) — main dish

gazpacho (gos PAH choh) — a cold soup made with tomatoes, green peppers, onions, celery; sometimes highly seasoned

maitre d' (MAY ter DEE) — the headwaiter in a fancy restaurant, usually a man; if a woman, she is called a "hostess" or the "maitre d' "

mousse (MOOSE) — a molded chilled dessert, often chocolate

paté (pah TAY) — finely chopped meat served as a dip or spread, often chicken livers; "paté de foie gras" — (pah TAY duh FWAH GRAH) is goose liver

pureed (pooh RAYED) — a paste or thick liquid; pureed vegetables are often put into soup

sherbet (SHER bet, not "SHER bert") — a cold dessert usually made with gelatin, milk and fruit juice

table d'hôte (TAH bull DOE) — you pay one price for the meal; this may then include soup, salad, vegetable *and* main dish

20

Tipping

The word "tipping" comes from the first letters of the words "to insure promptness." The idea was that you would be willing pay a little extra for really good service. Today, most service people expect a tip, and are very disappointed if they don't get one. Here are some tips on tipping.

Expected rates. In beauty shops and in restaurants in the United States, a tip of 15%-20% of the bill is now common. Taxi-drivers expect the same. Porters or bell-hops expect 50¢ per bag. You tip restroom attendants 25¢-50¢. In a beauty shop, if an operator (other than the one who later styles your hair) shampoos your hair, tip the shampooer at least $1.00. Take this into consideration when you tip the stylist.

Shaky arithmetic. With tipping, practice helps. To calculate a 15% tip easily, first divide the total amount of the bill by 10%. (Merely move the decimal point one place to the left. 10% of $10.00 is $1.00, of $10.50 is $1.05, etc.) Then add half of that amount to the original 10%. For a bill of $10.00, a 15% tip is $1.50: 10% of $10.00 is $1.00, and half of that is $.50, making a total of $1.50. By the way, calculate your tip on the amount BEFORE taxes. If a tip comes out to an odd number, say $1.58, most people do not make it exact. They leave $1.60.

Not satisfied. If you are dissatisfied with the service, do not leave the customary 15%-20% tip. You can leave a smaller amount, or none at all. Most people leave a smaller amount.

At the counter. If you are served at a counter, tip at least 25¢.

LOOKING THROUGH THE OTHER PERSON'S EYES

You never get a second chance to make a first impression.
Mark Twain

Throughout your life, you are going to be faced with unforeseen, ticklish situations. You may not think of them in terms of manners, but the way you handle yourself in these everyday situations says a lot about you. Do you know how to be polite when . . .

Through no fault of you own, you are late for a baby-sitting job.

Suppose you're with friends on the shopping trip. Your watch has stopped and you don't know it. Suddenly you realize that you cannot possibly get to your neighbor's house to sit with her five-year-old at the time you promised. What should you do? Would it be better to get there as fast as you can, or take the time to call her and explain the situation?

TIP: To help you decide, take the neighbor's point of view. In most cases, she has a deadline, too — someone is coming for her at a certain time, or she promised to be somewhere (a wedding or a dinner party) and promptness is important. You may not know what her deadline is but you can be sure she had a reason for setting the time for you to come.

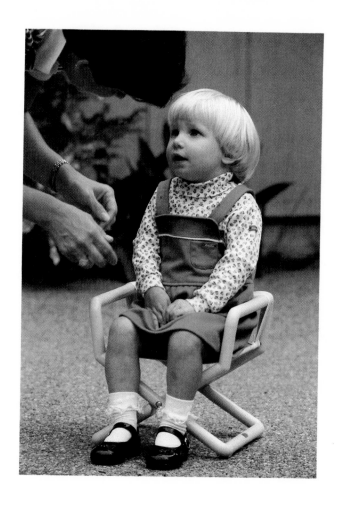

Caring for a youngster is serious business. Don't take babysitting lightly.

Call her and let her know that you are coming, though you'll be late. She may be able to make a temporary arrangement until you arrive. At least, she won't have to sit there wondering whether or not you are coming at all.

If you call ahead, your apology is likely to be more understandable. Even if she is still not too happy about your lateness, your behavior will show that you are aware of her needs and feelings.

Your boyfriend wants to snuggle in public.

Sometimes people try to use etiquette to persuade you to do something you don't want to do. Being polite doesn't mean that you have to do what someone wants, regardless of your own wishes. If your boyfriend wants a more intimate

24

expression of love than you're comfortable with, or a friend wants you to do something that you know is wrong, stand up for your rights. Anyone who tries to "use" you doesn't love you, or even like you.

A good friend's mother or father dies.

Expressing sympathy can be difficult for everyone. If a friend's parent or other loved one should die, and the household is one you visit frequently, chances are you will be able to express your feeling directly — both to your friend and the bereaved parent. This is the hard part for most of us. It often seems easier to do nothing at all, rather than take the chance of doing the "wrong" thing.

> **TIP**: Put yourself in the other person's place. Think how much it would mean to you to hear from your friends at such a time. Imagine how badly you would feel if you heard nothing at all. If you think it's hard for you to find the right words, remember that it can't possibly be as difficult as what your friend and her family are going through.

If you can't bring yourself to express sympathy in person, try writing a letter. Sometimes people can express feelings in print which are all but impossible to show personally. Mention some way in which the deceased person helped you, perhaps in a way that no one else knew about. If you're really tongue-tied, add a sentence or two to a store-bought card.

HOW DO YOU ACT
WHEN THINGS GET DIFFICULT?

Balancing your own needs and, at the same time, being polite is not always easy. How would you handle the situations given below? Remember: You want to maintain a good relationship but still be true to your own needs.

Your sister (or roommate) does not cooperate in cleaning up.

It can be difficult to get cooperation on cleaning up. You may already have tried the usual: suggestions, repeated suggestions, threats, humor, pleading. You may need to enlist your parents' help, but that can be tricky. You don't want to find yourself in the middle of a war between your parents and your sister. And parents, too, are sometimes less than successful in the "clean-up-your-room" battle.

Try to settle the problem between yourselves before it reaches crisis proportions. In stating your case, concentrate on the positive — it's more pleasant to live in a clean room than a hovel that looks like something out of a horror movie. Try not to be too critical. Above all, do not attack the problem as a personality defect. That will put your roommate on the defensive.

Get specific. What items are lost? Whose clothes were thrown all over the room? What books were borrowed and not returned to their proper places? You may be surprised that her response is that she didn't realize how you felt. Some people seem to be naturally neater than other people. Often the sloppy person does not realize how much stress her messiness is causing. Arriving at a solution you both can live with may take time. Good luck!

The conversation or jokes in a group become racist, sexist, or objectionable in some other way.

Objectionable talk is probably something you can deal with on a one-to-one basis with a friend. Depending on the friend and the depth of your friendship, you can be honest about your feelings. Or you can even discuss the problem in a small group. In a larger group you may not be able to express yourself as freely, unless you happen to know the group's attitudes. Even then, if you disagree, it may be a difficult time for you. All of us hate to lose friends or make enemies. It may be possible to show how you feel by not smiling or joining in the laughs. In time, you may become known as a person who does not make jokes at the expense of someone's race or ethnic background. In the meantime, you can just excuse yourself.

One person in a group behaves aggressively toward another member of the group.

We live in an imperfect world. Everyone does not receive an equal handout of brains, beauty, or riches. Humans sometimes feel jealous of one another. They want to strike back at those persons that they think make them feel unhappy. They sometimes embroider the truth in order to feel happier about themselves and sometimes persuade themselves that conflict (even war!) can answer their needs for revenge. What does this have to do with the world a teen-aged girl knows? It is hard to admit, but it is true that all of us have to learn to curb negative feelings about others. It follows that, from time to time, we also may need to help others do so.

So if one person — or even several — in your group acts in unfriendly ways to another, you may decide it is time to say you are not comfortable when this happens.

TIP: It is never easy to stand up to others in a group. It means you may lose one or several of the group members as friends. However, it is a gamble you may have to take if you want to stay true to your best self.

Some members of your group want to play a practical joke on someone.

Some practical jokes are very funny. When this is true and when the person on whom the joke is played is unhurt and also enjoys the joke, the joke is fine. It is equally true that some practical jokes are, at best, sick jokes — misguided attempts to be funny. They may end harmlessly, but it is also possible that they may not. If harm could come to another person, you would not want to be part of such a joke. Even if the harm isn't physical but only affects that person's self-esteem, you would not want to play a part in that either. It is hard to put a value on these kinds of damage. Who's to say that loss of self-esteem is less important — or more important — than physical hurt?

28

You will be able to judge the merits of a practical joke after you give it some thought.

The person assigned to drive you home has been drinking. You are at a party. Suppose a friend's brother arrives to drive you and your friend home. He has been at another party where he obviously drank beer rather freely. The way he is acting shows this quite clearly.

If possible, ask your friend to stay at the party longer and then call your parents or some other responsible person to come for you. Under the circumstances, do this as quietly and privately as you can. Take your friend aside and tell her that you think it is too risky to ride with her brother.

As a last resort, your friend might call her parents for help. Many communities now have active programs stressing the consequences of drinking and driving. This means there is greater awareness of the driver's responsibility and an acceptance of responsibility by parents or others. If chaperons or other adults are available, you may need to ask their advice. **Don't allow anyone who is drunk to drive you home. Being polite does not mean having to risk your life.**

At the beginning of this book we said that good manners are based on the Golden Rule. To sum up, then, one way to be more certain of your own rules of behavior is to try to think how other persons will be affected by the way you act. If you do this, it is more than likely that, in return, you will be treated fairly and politely by others. Even if that doesn't happen, don't give up! Learning good manners is a long and bumpy road for some of us. Be patient — with yourself and with the rest of us.

BIBLIOGRAPHY

"The Business of Etiquette," Patricia Leigh Brown. The New York Times Magazine. May 21, 1989.

Etiquette, Jr., Mary Elizabeth Clark and Margery Closey Quigley. Doubleday and Company, Inc., Garden City, NY.

Everyday Manners for Every Situation, Jennifer Crichton (assisted by the editors of Seventeen). Triangle Communications, Inc.

Manners Can Be Fun, Munro Leaf. J.B. Lippincott, New York; Reissued by Harper & Row, New York.

Miss Manners, Judith Martin. Warner Books, Inc., New York.

Emily Post's Etiquette, Elizabeth L. Post. Harper & Row, Publishers, New York, 14th Revised Edition.

"The New Etiquette: Be nice for the '90s," Laurence Sombke. USA Weekend. June 16-18, 1989.

The Amy Vanderbilt Complete Book of Etiquette, Amy Vanderbilt. Doubleday, Garden City, NY.

Mind Your Manners [board game] Question & Answers Guide. Baron/Scott Enterprises, Inc., Columbia, MD.

INDEX